MW00901606

"You are unique and special! ...Just like everyone else on this crazy planet."

"Today is a new day! ...
Full of the same anxieties as
yesterday."

"Be present in the moment! ...Unless there's a good movie on TV."

"You are capable of amazing things!
...But probably not today."

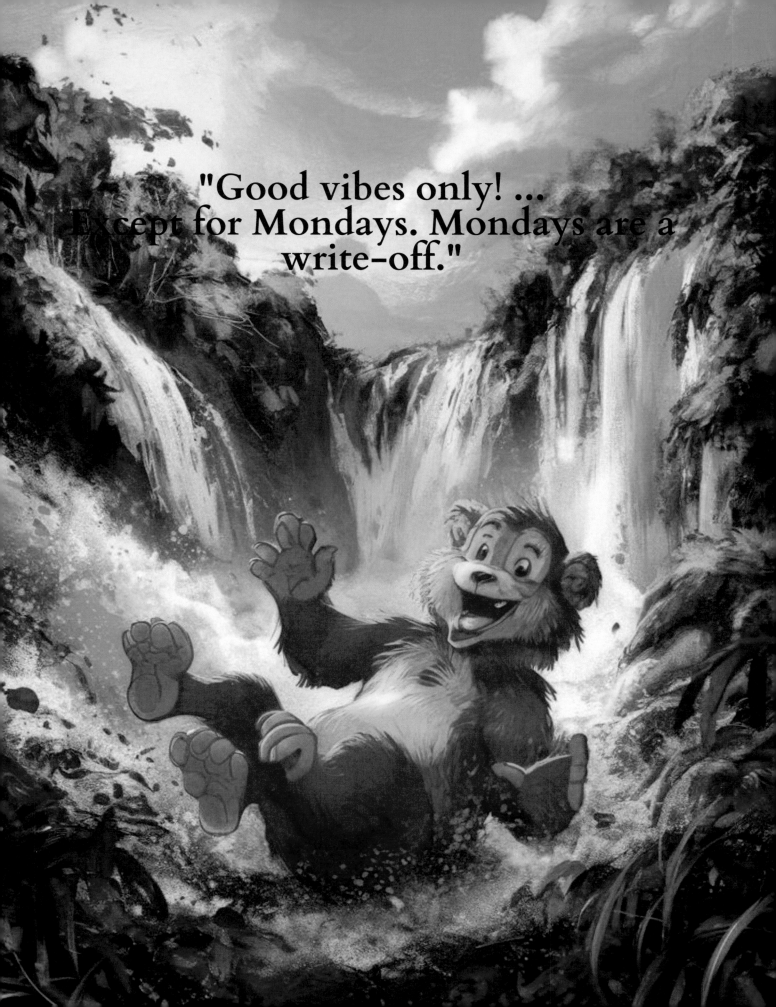

"Multitasking is a superpower! Unless you're trying to cook dinner and fold laundry at the same time. Then it's a recipe for disaster."

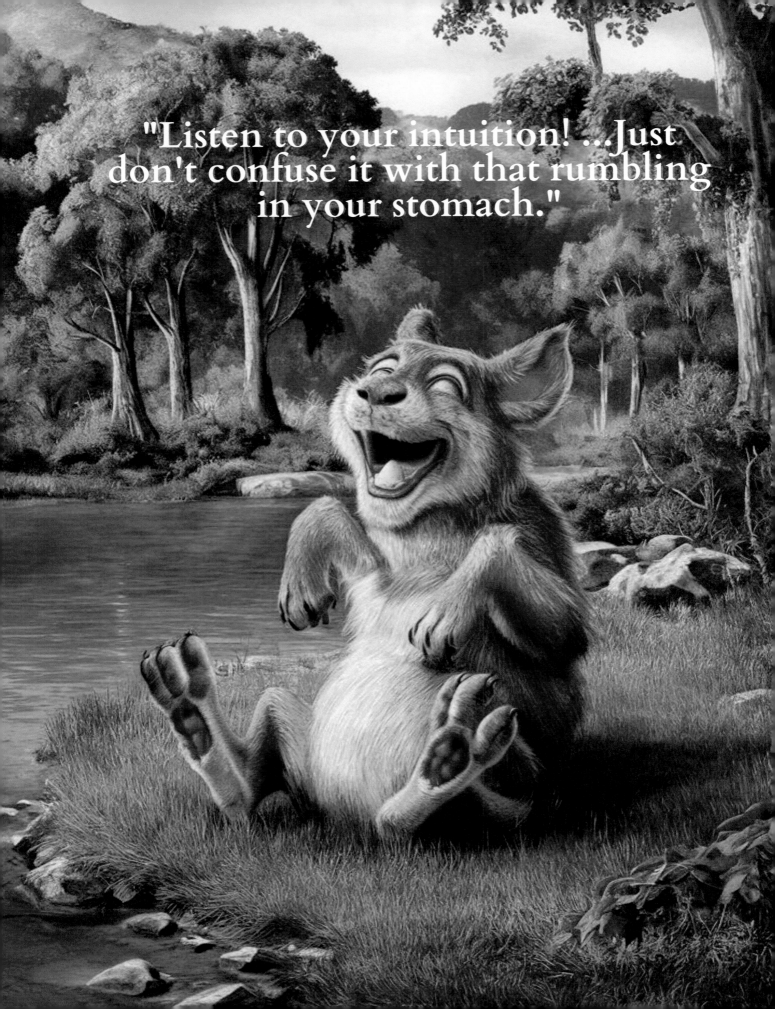

"Adulting is easy! ...Just kidding, nobody knows what they're doing."

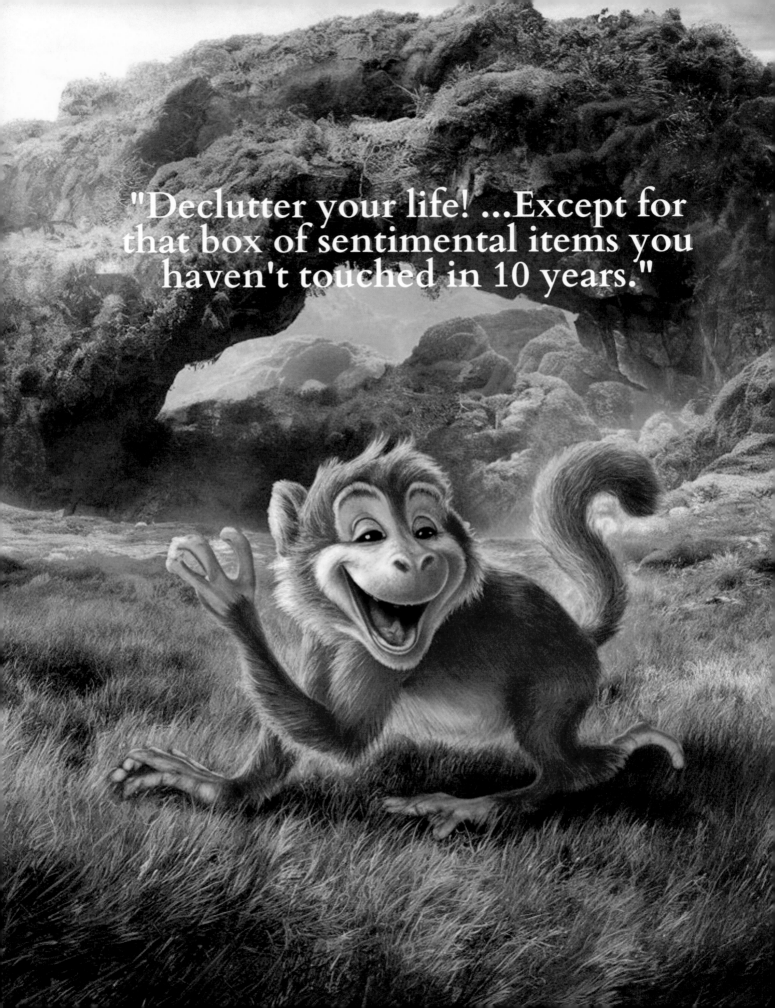

"Declutter your life! ...Except for that box of sentimental items you haven't touched in 10 years."

"Early bird gets the worm...But the night owl gets the good sleep."

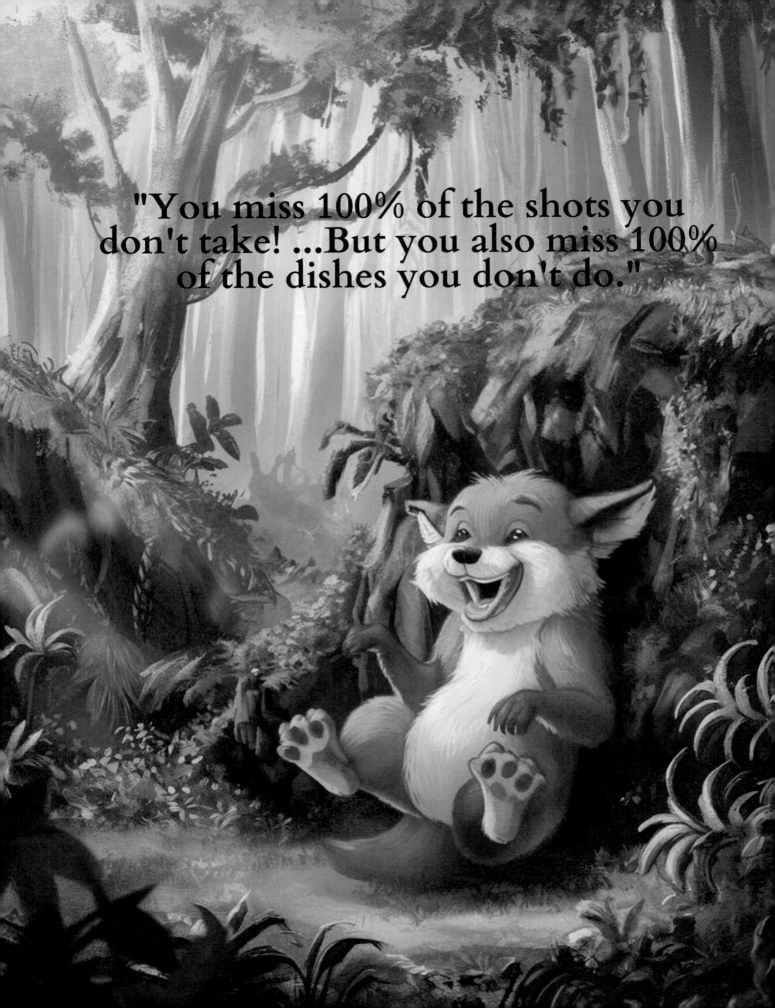

"Be the change you want to see in the world! ...Just don't expect the world to change overnight."

"You are your biggest cheerleader!
...Unless your best friend is Beyonce.
Then it's Beyonce."

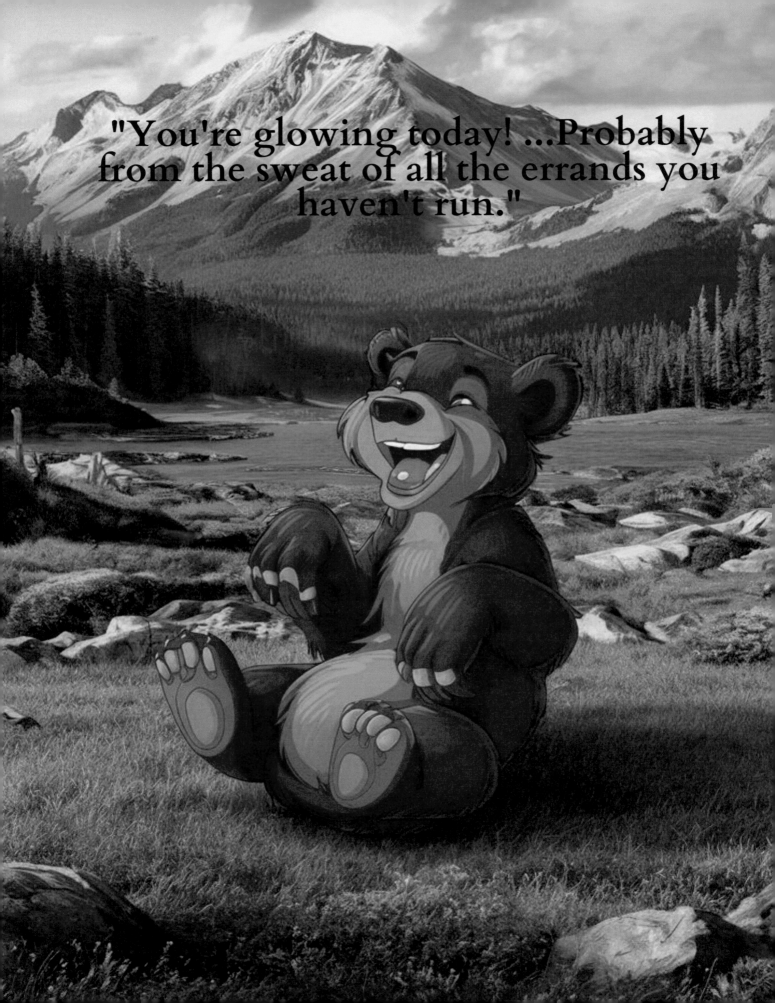

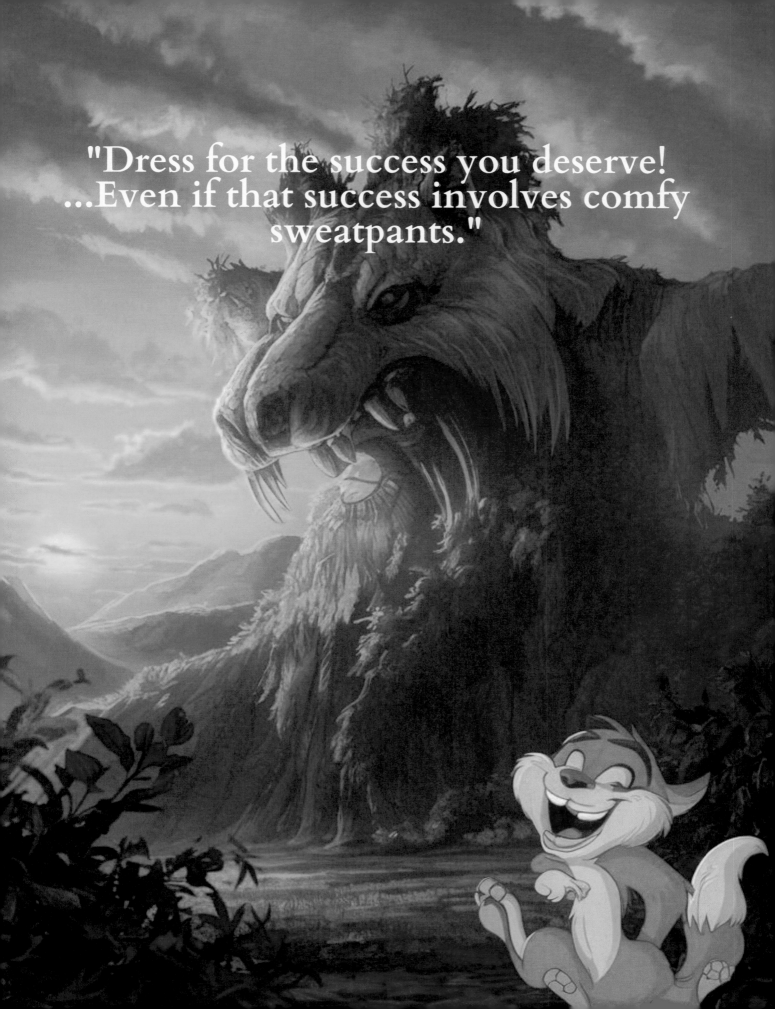

"Dress for the success you deserve!
...Even if that success involves comfy
sweatpants."

Made in United States
Troutdale, OR
10/01/2024